MW01717295

This Book Belongs To:

____

____

____

Published by Anglican House Media Ministry, Inc., Newport Beach, California. You may contact us online at www.anglicanhousemedia.org. Printed by Asia Printing Co., Ltd., Seoul, Korea. Text set in Baskerville typeface.

Anglican House
Media Ministry

ISBN 978-0-9970167-2-7

The Nicene Creed

Illustrated and Instructed

For Kids

For my wife.

I love you Brandie with all of my heart. Thank you for standing with me through it all.

To my children Sam, Jack, Luke, and Lila:

Let this amazing faith, handed down from generation to generation, lead you to your Heavenly Father's outstretched arms. I am proud to be your Dad.

CONTENTS

About The Author

Photo by Holly Bracy

Joey Fitzgerald is a priest in the Anglican Church of North America and is the Rector of the Church of the Outer Banks in Nags Head, NC. He and his wife Brandie are the parents of four children: Sam, Jack, Luke, and Lila. Before he was ordained, Joey taught art in public schools. He enjoys using art as a tool in sharing the Gospel of Jesus.

Dear Reader,

For over 1600 years the Nicene Creed has been the standard of orthodoxy across Christian traditions. It anchors our faith by stating the essential beliefs of Christianity. Written in 325 A.D. at the Council of Nicea, and finalized in 381 A.D. at the Council of Constantinople, the Creed corrected a heresy that denied the divinity of Jesus Christ. The deception that Jesus Christ is not God, but only a good man, lives on today in many who profess to follow Christ. By believing and reciting the Scriptural truths found in the words of the Creed, we safeguard ourselves from false beliefs that lead us away from God.

It is our responsibility to teach God's truths to our children. They are full members of the church too, and they deserve to know the good news of the Gospel. That is why God says of his words:

"Make them known to your children and your children's children."
DEUTERONOMY 4:9

The Nicene Creed truly is a remarkable document! It is deeply faithful to Holy Scripture, God's Word; succinct, yet fully expressive of the Christian faith. It unifies us in the midst of today's individualistic culture. It is an act of heart-forming worship of the One True God. As we say the Nicene Creed, we are reminded that God is Triune: One God, but *three persons.* The Father is glorified, Christ is exalted, and the Holy Spirit is invited.

My hope and prayer is that this book for the edification of children will be the first step in a new generation's unpacking the treasures of God's Truth. Read it with your children, talk about it. There are scripture references throughout, so you can grab a Bible and dig in further if you like.

This is our faith. I hope that you hand it down!

Peace and Blessings,
Rev. Joey Fitzgerald

A Note on the Christian Creeds

The Creeds acknowledged in Christendom are the Athanasian Creed, the Apostles' Creed, and the Nicene Creed. Of these the most widely used is the Nicene Creed.

What is a creed?

A creed is a statement of faith. The word "creed" comes from the Latin credo, meaning "I believe." JOHN 20:24-29

What is the purpose of the Creeds?

The purpose of the Creeds is to declare and safeguard God's truth about himself, about ourselves, and about creation, as God has revealed it in Holy Scripture. 2 PETER 1:19-2; JOHN 20:31

What does belief in the Creeds signify?

Belief in the Creeds signifies acceptance of God's revealed truth, and the intention to live by it. 2 TIMOTHY 3:14-15

Why do Christians acknowledge these creeds?

You acknowledge them together with the Church because they are grounded in Holy Scripture and are faithful expressions of its teaching. 1 CORINTHIANS 15:3-11; PHILIPPIANS 2:6-11

Why should you know these Creeds?

You should know these Creeds because they state the essential beliefs of the Christian faith.

Note: These questions and answers are taken from: *To Be A Christian: An Anglican Catechism.* Anglican House Publishers, 2014. ISBN 978-0-9860441-2-0

Why Share the Creed with Children?

You might be asking yourself why you should take the time to teach children about The Nicene Creed. Is it really that important?

The answer is absolutely yes! The Nicene Creed states the essence of God's truths, as revealed in Holy Scripture. And Holy Scripture makes it perfectly clear that young children are to be taught the truths of God:

"the Lord said to me, 'Gather the people to me, that I may let them hear my words, so that they may learn to fear me all the days that they live on the earth, and that they may teach their children so.'" DEUTERONOMY 4:10

"You shall teach them to your children, talking of them when you are sitting in your house, and when you are walking by the way, and when you lie down, and when you rise." DEUTERONOMY 11:19

Even the youngest child has an inborn longing to connect with God's truths, which are fully revealed in Jesus Christ. And Jesus certainly wants to connect with each child:

" Now they were bringing even infants to him that he might touch them. And when the disciples saw it, they rebuked them. But Jesus called them to him, saying, "Let the children come to me, and do not hinder them, for to such belongs the kingdom of God. Truly, I say to you, whoever does not receive the kingdom of God like a child shall not enter it." LUKE 18:15-17

There are many promises connected with the Lord's admonitions, and this particular promise concerning children is perfectly clear:

"Train up a child in the way he should go; even when he is old he will not depart from it." PROVERBS 22:6

When we are teaching God's truths, children will ask amazingly penetrating and powerful questions! With this in mind, we have included **Keywords For Kids**. It's a glossary of word meanings for children, together with one or more examples for each word. (It's a pretty good idea to have a good look at it before using the book with your children or students!)

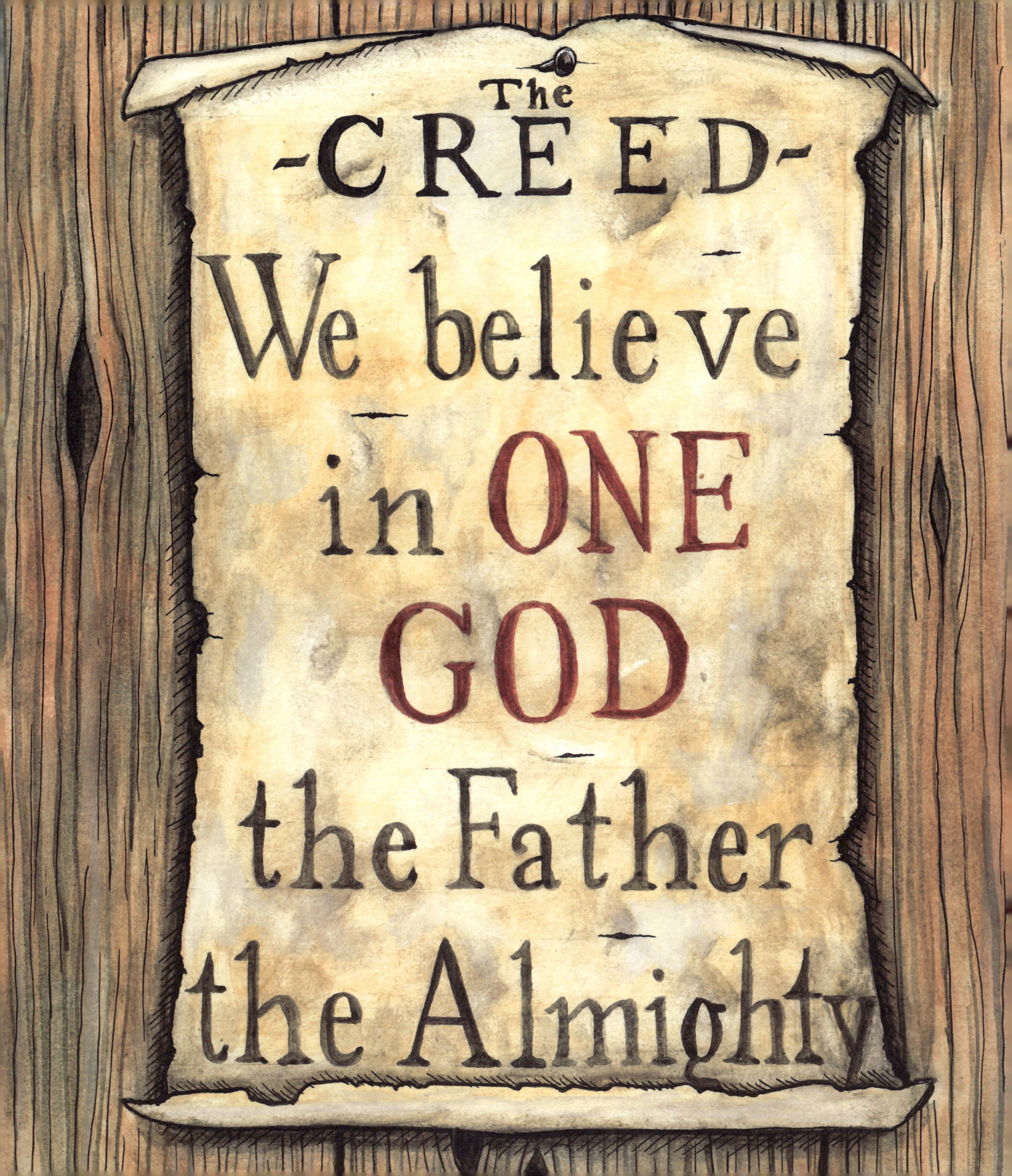
The
-CREED-
We believe
in ONE
GOD
the Father
the Almighty

We believe in one God,
the Father, the Almighty,
maker of heaven and earth,
of all that is, visible and invisible.

God is completely unique. There has never been anyone like him, and there never will be! ISAIAH 45:5-6 God does not have a beginning, and he does not have an end. PSALM 90:2 God is the Creator of everything that exists. He made things we can see, like the sun, the moon, and the stars. He made chickens, llamas, cucumbers, baby sisters, and bananas. He even created the things we can't see, like music, our thought, angels, Heaven, and our spirits. GENESIS 1

God loves all of his creation very much! However, it is his people that he loves the most. He lovingly made you and all people. He created us in his image and wants us to be his children. That is why we call him "Father." GENESIS 2; GALATIONS 4:4-7

We believe in one Lord, Jesus Christ,
the only Son of God,
eternally begotten of the Father,
God from God, Light from Light,
true God from true God,
begotten, not made,
of one Being with the Father,
through him all things were made.

Jesus is the Son of the Father. MATTHEW 3:17 This doesn't mean that God the Father created Jesus. There was never a time when Jesus was not there! When the Father was dreaming about the world he wanted to make, Jesus was dreaming with him. JOHN 1:1-5 Before they made you they thought about every single little detail. They knew what color of hair they wanted you to have, what color of skin; if you would be tall or short, big or small. And they loved you then as much as they do now.

When the Nicene Creed says that Jesus Christ is "Light from Light" and "True God from True God," it means that Jesus and the Father are both God. Jesus is not just the *son* of God, he is God *the Son*. It is because the Father and the Son love the world so much that God the Son came to Earth.

For us and for our salvation
he came down from heaven,
was incarnate from the
Holy Spirit and the Virgin Mary,
and was made man.

The Incarnation is a fancy way of saying that God the Son became a human too. He was born as a baby, just like you. His earthly parents Mary and Joseph named him Jesus. LUKE 2:1-21 He had skin, hair, arms, legs, fingers and toes! He learned to walk and talk, and to read and write. He played with friends, swam in rivers, helped Joseph work as a carpenter, learned in the synagogue, and grew up to be an amazing person! LUKE 2:41-52 Jesus is all God and he is all man! LUKE 24:39, PHILIPIANS 3:21

Why was it so important for God the Son to become a human being and come to Earth? When God made the first people, Adam and Eve, they disobeyed him. GENESIS 3 Disobeying God is called sin, and no one is free from it. ROMANS 3:23 We have all disobeyed God in our own way. Sin keeps us away from God. God is the creator of all life. If we are separated from him, we can't have the life that he wants for us on Earth or forever with him in Heaven. God wants us to be with him and to have life! This is why Jesus came; to forgive us our sins, to give us life, and to rescue the whole world. ROMANS 6:23 This is called salvation, and it is a free gift that God gives to all who believe in him! ROMANS 1:16

For our sake he was crucified
under Pontius Pilate;
he suffered death and was buried.
On the third day he rose again
in accordance with the Scriptures;

Salvation comes to us because Jesus is both a man and God! When he died on the cross, he took away our sins. 1PETER 2:24 Jesus' friends were sad and afraid. They didn't understand what Jesus had to do. They hid in a room from Friday until Sunday. JOHN 20:19 That's when something really amazing happened...

Jesus rose from the grave! We call this the ressurection. He was there, with the apostles, the other disciples, and family, fully alive! 1CORINTHIANS 15:3-8 People from all over Israel saw him. He spoke to them, walked with them, and even sat down at a table and ate food with them.

When Jesus died and rose again, he defeated death completely. Now you and I, and anyone who follows him, can live forever with God! JOHN 3:16 And we don't even have to wait until we get to Heaven to experience his power and love. It begins now, as soon as we start to follow him! JOHN 10:10

He ascended into heaven
and is seated at the right hand of the Father.
He will come again in glory to judge the living and the dead,
and his kingdom will have no end.

After Jesus rose, he spent time with his followers. He told them that he was going to go be with the Father, and he would send them a helper, God the Holy Spirit. After that, Jesus went up into Heaven to be with the Father. ACTS 1:1-11

Jesus promised that he would come back one day, but that only God the Father knows the day and the hour. MARK 13:32 When Jesus comes back, the Kingdom of God will be complete! We will have a new Heaven and a new Earth that will come together into one wonderful world! God's Kingdom is totally perfect. There will be no tears, no pain, and no death, and God's people will experience real, unending life! REVELATION 21:1-4

is not
THE FATHER
THE SON
is
is
GOD
is not
is not
is
THE HOLY SPIRIT

We believe in the Holy Spirit, the Lord,
the giver of life,
who proceeds from the Father
[and the Son],

We have already said that the Father and the Son are both God. Even though there is only One God, he is made up of three separate persons. This is called the Trinity. The Holy Spirit is the third person of God. JOHN 14:26

This can be really confusing. Sometimes pictures can help us to better understand complicated ideas. The picture on the opposite page is called the Shield of the Trinity. Christians a long time ago drew pictures like this to help them understand how God could be three persons in One God.

Look at the symbol for the Holy Spirit. The symbol is a dove. Do you remember the story of when the Holy Spirit descended like a dove on Jesus? MATTHEW 3:16 Follow the line from the dove to the middle. The Holy Spirit is God! If you follow the circle around, you will see that the Holy Spirit is not the Father, and he is not the Son. However, together, all three make the One True God. The fullness of God is in each person of the Holy Trinity.

Each member of the Trinity has a unique role. The Holy Spirit's job is to comfort us, and remind us to always look to Jesus as our Lord. The Holy Spirit fills us with God's power. In the Holy Spirit we are joined to God and to other Christians! JOHN 16:7-15, EPHESIANS 4:4

Who with the Father and the Son is worshiped and glorified, who has spoken through the prophets.

The Holy Spirit has always been with the Father and the Son, and he helped the Father and the Son to create our universe. GENESIS 1:1-2 Through the Holy Spirit, God has spoken to the world through his people, Scripture, and the Church. Before Jesus died, rose, and ascended into Heaven, the Holy Spirit only came to a few people and at special times. Now, the Holy Spirit has been poured out and he is at work around us everyday. ACTS 2:17, JOHN 15:26, JOHN 16 7-15 As you will find out, the Holy Spirit can work through you, too!

Jesus said that if we have faith in him, we can experience the power of his Kingdom now, even doing the same things that Jesus did. JOHN 14:12-14 We can do that because the Holy Spirit fills us with love, joy, peace, patience, kindness, goodness, faithfulness, gentleness, and self-control, and all sorts of other good gifts. GALATIONS 5:22-23, 1 CORINTHIANS 12:8-10 He does this to help us be more like Jesus and to faithfully serve the Kingdom of God!

We believe in one holy catholic and apostolic Church. We acknowledge one baptism for the forgiveness of sins.

Jesus told his followers they would receive power when the Holy Spirit came. After Jesus returned to Heaven to be with the Father, the Holy Spirit came upon the Apostles, and many of Jesus' other followers, just as Jesus promised. ACTS 1:8, 2:1-4 Immediately, they began to tell other people about his death, resurrection, and the love of the Father! These people became the first Church. The Church includes all the people who have ever followed Jesus, and all those who will follow him in the future, no matter where, or when they live! MATTHEW 28:19

Baptism shows that we are united with Christ in his death and in his resurrection. ROMANS 6:1-11 Jesus was baptized by John the Baptist, and Jesus commanded his followers to baptize others in the name of the Father and of the Son and of the Holy Spirit. MATTHEW 3:1-17, 28:19-20 When we are baptized, we confess that we will follow Jesus and we reject Satan and all evil things. We also confess that we believe all that the Bible teaches, and that we will be obedient to God's teaching and commandments.

We look for the resurrection of the dead, and the life of the world to come. Amen.

One day, this world will end, but our lives will go on forever in God's Kingdom of the new Heaven and new Earth. All those who have become adopted children of God, through Jesus, will live in this new world, and it will never, ever end! There will be feasts, parties, friends, families, angels, and so much more! REVELATION 21 Best of all, God will be with us, Father, Son, and Holy Spirit!

When we follow Jesus, these are the things we agree to believe. It is not always easy, but through God's grace, we can choose to follow him even when it is hard. This is called faith, and, when we have faith in God, he will never leave us!

Are you ready to believe the words of the Nicene Creed and to have faith?

Are you ready to experience the love of God, starting right now?

Whenever you are ready, you can close your eyes, and say a prayer like this:

"Dear God, I believe in Jesus Christ. I want to give my life to him, and experience the love of the Father, the grace of the Son, and have the Holy Spirit fill me with his peace."

Amen!

Life of the Worl

to come.

The Nice

We believe in one God,
the Father, the Almighty,
maker of heaven and earth,
of all that is, visible and invisible.

We believe in one Lord, Jesus Christ,
the only Son of God,
eternally begotten of the Father,
God from God, Light from Light,
true God from true God,
begotten, not made,
of one Being with the Father;
through him all things were made.
For us and for our salvation he came down from heaven,
was incarnate from the Holy Spirit and the Virgin Mary,
and was made man.
For our sake he was crucified under Pontius Pilate;
he suffered death and was buried.
On the third day he rose again in accordance with the Scriptures;
He ascended into heaven
and is seated at the right hand of the Father.
He will come again in glory to judge the living and the dead,
and his kingdom will have no end.

ne Creed

We believe in the Holy Spirit, the Lord, the giver of life,
who proceeds from the Father [and the Son].
who with the Father and the Son is worshiped and
glorified, who has spoken through the prophets.
We believe in one holy catholic and apostolic Church.
We acknowledge one baptism for the forgiveness of sins.
We look for the resurrection of the dead,
and the life of the world to come. Amen.

Note: 1. Some traditions use the singular *I Believe* rather than the plural *We Believe*.
2. The phrase known as the *filioque* [and the Son] is not in the original Greek text.
Nevertheless, in the Western Church, the *filioque* [and the Son] is customary in worship.

Keywords for Kids

Word	Meaning	Example(s)
Almighty	Able to do things that no one else can do	Only God is all powerful!
Amen	To agree with something	Jesus loves you! Amen!
Apostles	Jesus' closest 12 disciples	Peter, Andrew, James, John, Philip, Bartholomew, Simon, Thomas, Thaddaeus, James, Matthew, and Judas. Later, Paul became an apostle too!
Apostolic	What the Apostles learned from Jesus and taught others.	Some of the apostles wrote most of the books and letters of the New Testament.
Ascension	Going up	A balloon can ascend (go up) in the sky.
Baptism	Being presented to Jesus and adopted into God's Family.	Jesus was baptized in water by John the Baptist in the Jordan River.
Begotten	Having a daddy	Jesus' daddy is God the Father.
Believe	Trusting that what we know is really true	We trust and know that Jesus loves us very much!
Catholic	Something that is all around the world	Jesus' church is all over the world.
Christ	Jesus' title and job	Jesus is the Christ, the savior of the world!

Keywords for Kids

Word	Meaning	Example(s)
Creed	Words that describe what we believe	We believe that Jesus died for our sins and opens Heaven to all who believe.
Crucified	Killed on a cross	Long ago, Roman soldiers would crucify criminals.
Eternal	No beginning and no end, for ever and ever	God is eternal and we will live with him in Heaven for ever and ever!
Forgiveness	Letting go of feelings that have been hurt	We forgive someone when we let go of our hurt feelings and just love them.
Glorified	Lifted up and placed where all can see	A trophy is placed on shelf so that everyone can see it.
Grace	God's favor to us, free and undeserved	Grace is the means by which we receive God's loving care for us.
God	The Creator of the World, who has always been and will always be	God has three persons: God the Father, God the Son, and God the Holy Spirit.
Gospel	Good news	The God news of Jesus as told in the Bible, specifically in Matthew, Mark, Luke, and John.

Keywords for Kids

Word	Meaning	Example(s)
Heaven	God's home	Even though we can't see it, it is just as real as where you are, only better!
Holy	Made his own by God	We are made Holy because God has adopted us as his children.
Holy Spirit	He is theThird Person of the Trinity	The Holy Spirit helps us to love others and he turns our hearts to Jesus.
Incarnate	Having a real body	When Jesus came to earth, he had a real body with skin, hair and everything!
Invisible	Something that can't be looked at with our eyes	The wind, our thoughts, and music are all unseen, but very real.
Jesus	The second Person of the Trinity	Jesus is God, the Son of the Father.
Kingdom	The land and people that a king is ruler of	God's Kingdom is in Heaven and on Earth.
Pontius Pilate	A Roman ruler who lived in Israel	Pontius Pilate was in charge of Jesus' trial and ordered his death on the Cross.
Prophets	People that speak God's words to others.	Isaiah and John the Baptist were two of the prophets.

Keywords for Kids

Word	Meaning	Example(s)
Resurrection	Coming back to life after death	Jesus came back to life and prepares a place for us in His Kingdom for the day we are resurrected to new life!
Salvation	To be saved from something	We are saved, by Jesus, from eternal death!
Satan	The enemy who would lead us away from God	Satan wants us to ignore God.
Scriptures	The words of God in the Bible	Genesis, Psalms, and The Gospel of John are some books of the Bible
Sin	The things that keep us from God	When we disobey God and his desire for our lives.
Spirits	The invisible part of who we are.	In Heaven, God gives us new bodies for our spirits to live in.
Trinity	Three persons in One	God has three persons; Father, Son, and Holy Spirit, but he is ONE God.
Virgin Mary	Jesus' earthly mother	Mary had Jesus by a miracle of the Holy Spirit.
Worship	Giving love to God	We worship God when we show him love by singing, praying, and obeying him.

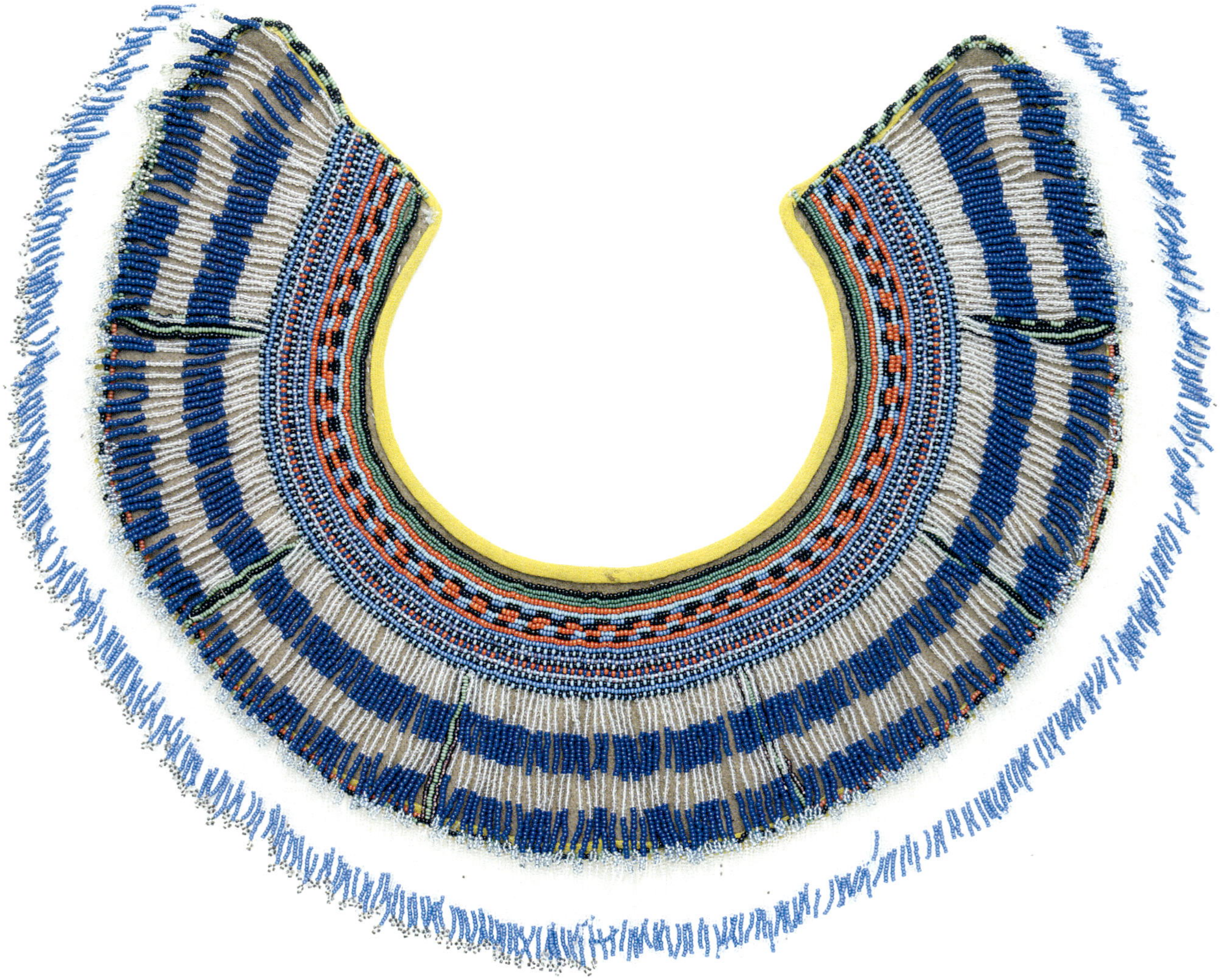

1

BEADED COLLAR 1969

2

BEADED COLLAR 1969

3

MANITOBA 1971

4

MY HOMELAND 1973

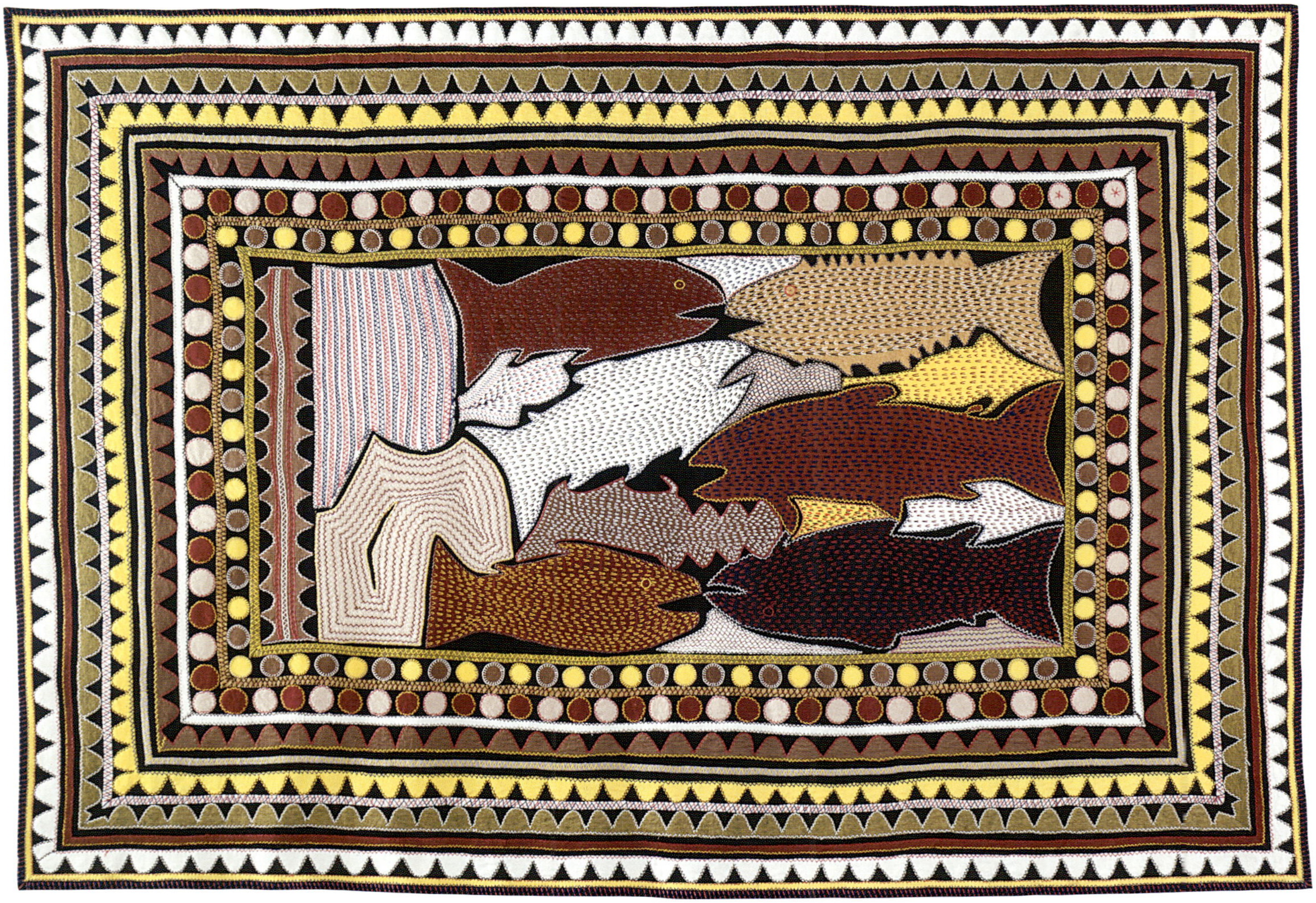

5

LAKE TROUT 1973

6

TRUMPETER SWANS 1973

7

NIGHT SKY 1974

8

HEARTS 1974

9

THIRTY FACES 1974

10

CROWD OF PEOPLE 1974

11

UNTITLED 1975

12

SUN WOMAN 1975

13

HAPPY FACE 1975

14

SEAL HUNT 1976

15

UNTITLED c. 1976

Detail, p. 49

16

SPRING 1976

17

ULU WOMEN 1976

18

TOGETHER IN SPRING 1977

19

LAUGHING AT MEN WITH BIG NOSES

1978

20

PEOPLE, SHAMANS, AND SPIRITS c. 1978

21

JOURNEY 1978

22

GOOSE HUNTING IN SPRING 1978

23

IMAGINING TREES 1978

24

THE LIFE OF A MAN c. 1978–79

25

FACES (FROM THE STORY OF KIVIUQ AND IQUPJUK) 1979

26

UNTITLED 1979

27

BOUNTIFUL THOUGHTS c. 1978–79

28

DISMEMBERED/REMEMBERED c. 1979–80

29

TELE-VISION SPIRITS c. 1980

30

COMPOSITION (LARGE BIRD AND FIGURES) c. 1981

31

UNTITLED c. 1983

32

AVAALAAQIAQ (WILLOWS) 1985

33

ONE MAN'S DREAM 1988

34

TUU'LUQ AND HER FAMILY 1988

35

UNTITLED 1989

36

THE PRAYER MEETING 1989

Tuu'luq and friend with *Rites of Spring*, 1989.
Photo: Marie Bouchard

37

RITES OF SPRING 1989

LIST OF WORKS IN THE EXHIBITION

For complete information on exhibitions and publications, see the Exhibitions and Public Collections list and the Selected Bibliography. Page references at the end of each entry are to discussions of the work in this catalogue.

A Note on Materials

Tuu'luq's works on cloth were produced using one of two fabrics for the background support. These have in themselves interesting hybrid histories as colonial trade goods.

Duffle (named after the Belgian town of Duffel) is a coarse woollen cloth with a thick nap. It has been used in Europe and North America since at least the 1600s as a fabric to make warm clothing resistant to the elements. When imported into the Arctic by traders such as the Hudson's Bay Company, it began to be used by Inuit to make, among other things, cloth versions of traditional skin garments. For example, an *amauti* (woman's parka) was designed using duffle for the inner layer and canvas for the outer covering. This type of amauti is still being made today.

Stroud (named after the town in England where it was made) is a thinner, cheaper, primarily woollen cloth with a similar dense nap that has also been in existence since the 1600s. First manufactured from woollen rags, it was made expressly for barter or sale in trading with the aboriginal peoples of North America. A trade blanket manufactured of this material was also known as a stroud.

Onto these duffle and stroud supports, Tuu'luq used embroidery and other threads to hand-sew shapes cut from a third material, felt.

Felt, unlike duffle and stroud, is not woven. Felt is formed by combining wool (and sometimes other fibres, such as fur and hair) with a sizing liquid. This mixture is then pressed and rolled into a compact substance which, because of its construction, does not fray at the edges when cut. This characteristic makes it highly suitable for appliqué work.

1
Beaded Collar 1969
Glass beads, thread, wool, and stroud
17.7 cm wide from inside neck to edge of fringe; 106.0 cm outside circumference; 53.0 cm wide overall
Glenbow Museum, Calgary (AB 1390)
(see text pp. 27, 28, 35, 36, 99)

2
Beaded Collar 1969
Glass beads, thread, stroud, bias tape, antler buttons and sinew button loops
19.5 cm from inside neck to edge of fringe; 111.0 cm outside circumference; 56.0 cm wide overall
Collection Sheila Butler and Jack Butler, London, Ontario
(see text pp. 27, 28, 35, 36, 99)

3
Manitoba 1971
Felt, embroidery floss, and thread on stroud
87.0 x 51.0 cm
Art Gallery of Ontario, Toronto. Gift of George Swinton, 1990 (90/350, formerly *Faces and Bears*)
(see text pp. 22, 28)

EXHIBITIONS
Sananguaq: The Swinton Collection, 1991
A Stitch in Time, 1997

4
My Homeland 1973
Felt, embroidery floss, and thread on duffle
135.0 x 94.0 cm
University of Alberta Art and Artifact Collection, Museums and Collections Services, Clifford E. Lee Collection of Inuit Wall Hangings, Edmonton (983.44.6, formerly *Untitled*)
(see text pp. 22, 31)

EXHIBITIONS
Tuu'luq/Anguhadluq, 1976 (no. 28 in catalogue, as *Untitled*, repr., n. p.)
Universiade '83, 1983
Clifford E. Lee Collection, 1984
Inuit Art in Edmonton Collections, 1985
Celebration of the Human Spirit, 1988
Marion Tuu'luq, 1990 (repr. on exhibition poster)
A University Collects, 1994
Arctic Survival, 2001–02

PUBLICATION
Ingram, 1990 (repr. p. 49)

5
Lake Trout 1973
Felt, embroidery floss, and thread on duffle
145.0 x 207.0 cm
Prince of Wales Northern Heritage Centre, Government of the Northwest Territories, Yellowknife (formerly *Untitled*)
(see text pp. 12, 36, 37, 42, 100)

EXHIBITIONS
Crafts from Arctic Canada, 1974 (no. 190 in catalogue, as *Untitled*, col. repr. p. 36)
Olympic Games, 1976
Tuu'luq/Anguhadluq, 1976 (probably no. 30 in catalogue, as *Untitled*)

PUBLICATION
Northward Journal 23 (repr. p. 22)

6
Trumpeter Swans 1973
Felt, embroidery floss, and thread on duffle
121.4 x 123.0 cm
Klamer Family Collection, Toronto
(see text pp. 34, 35)

EXHIBITIONS
Baker Lake Wall Hangings, 1973
Tuu'luq/Anguhadluq, 1976 (no. 33 in catalogue, as *Birds and Men*)
A Stitch in Time, 1997

PUBLICATION
Zazelenchuk, 1974 (repr. p. 2)

7
Night Sky 1974
Felt, embroidery floss, and thread on duffle
119.0 x 137.3 cm
Inscriptions: b.c. in embroidery floss, "Tuu'luq" (in syllabics)
Bank of Montreal, Toronto
(see text p. 38)

EXHIBITIONS
Tuu'luq/Anguhadluq, 1976 (no. 31 in catalogue, as *Transformations*)
Between Worlds, 1994
A Stitch in Time, 1997

8
Hearts 1974
Felt, embroidery floss, and thread on stroud
115.5 x 92.0 cm
Inscriptions: b.c. in embroidery floss, "Tuu'luq" (in syllabics)
Collection Robert and Irene Bilan, Winnipeg
(see text pp. 13, 30)

EXHIBITIONS
Tuu'luq/Anguhadluq, 1976 (no. 32 in catalogue, repr., n. p.)
Northern Lights, 1994 (no. 29 in catalogue, repr. p. 55)

9
Thirty Faces 1974
Felt, embroidery floss, and thread on stroud
141.0 x 124.0 cm
Inscriptions: b.c. in embroidery floss, "Tuu'luq" (in syllabics)
The Winnipeg Art Gallery (G-76-956)
(see text pp. 21, 28)

EXHIBITIONS
Tuu'luq/Anguhadluq, 1976 (no. 34 in catalogue, repr. on cover)
Immaginario Inuit, 1995 (no. 40 in catalogue, col. repr. p. 104)
R. C. A. Prairie Region Exhibition, 1997–98 (listed in catalogue, no number)

PUBLICATION
Northward Journal 23, repr. p. 23

10
Crowd of People 1974
Felt, embroidery floss, and thread on duffle
131.0 x 178.0 cm
Collection Stanley and Jean Zazelenchuk, St. Andrews, New Brunswick
(see text p. 40)

EXHIBITIONS
Tuu'luq/Anguhadluq, 1976 (no. 44 in catalogue, repr., n. p.)
A Stitch in Time, 1997

11
Untitled 1975
Felt, embroidery floss, and thread on stroud
208.0 x 136.0 cm
Inscriptions: b.l. in embroidery floss, "Tuu'luq" (in syllabics)
Private collection
(see text pp. 13, 28, 30, 36, 40)

EXHIBITIONS
Tuu'luq/Anguhadluq, 1976 (no. 45 in catalogue, as *Abstract*, repr., n. p.)
A Stitch in Time, 1997

12
Sun Woman 1975
Felt, embroidery floss, and thread on stroud
127.0 x 183.0 cm
Inscriptions: b.c. in embroidery floss, "Marion Tuu'luq" (in syllabics)
Art Gallery of Ontario, Toronto. Gift of the Klamer Family, 1978 (78/670)
(see text pp. 35, 101)

EXHIBITIONS
Tuu'luq/Anguhadluq, 1976 (no. 41 in catalogue)
Grasp Tight the Old Ways,1983 (no. 28 in catalogue, repr. p. 69, col. pl. p. 29)

PUBLICATIONS
Botkin and Keller, 1994 (col. repr. p. 30)
Newlands, 2000 (col. repr. p. 318)

13
Happy Face 1975
Felt, embroidery floss, and thread on stroud
127.0 x 85.0 cm
Inscriptions: b.c. in embroidery floss, "Marion Tuu'luq" (in syllabics)
Government of Manitoba Art Collection, Winnipeg (0360005, formerly *Untitled*)
(see text p. 34)

14
Seal Hunt 1976
Felt, embroidery floss, and thread on stroud
137.0 x 142.0 cm
Inscriptions: b.l. in embroidery floss, "Tuu'luq" (in syllabics)
Collection Martin and Shelley Tadman, Winnipeg
(see text p. 32)

EXHIBITIONS
Marion Tuu'luq, 1980 (no. 9 in booklet, as *#1500*, col. repr., n. p.)
Winnipeg Collects, 1987 (no. 143 in catalogue, as *Wallhanging*, repr. p. 37)

15
Untitled c. 1976
Felt, embroidery floss, and thread on duffle
122.0 x 103.5 cm
National Gallery of Canada, Ottawa. Gift of the Department of Indian Affairs and Northern Development, 1989 (36651)
(see text pp. 13, 31, 36, 38, 101)

EXHIBITIONS
In the Shadow of the Sun, 1988–90 (no. 272 in catalogue, as *Sednas Freigiebigkeit* [Sedna's Bounty], col. repr. p. 610)
Northern Lights, 1993–94 (no. 30 in catalogue, col. repr. p. 29)
National Gallery of Canada, 1998–99

PUBLICATIONS
Muehlen, 1989 (col. repr. on cover)

16
Spring 1976
Felt, embroidery floss, and thread on duffle
101.0 x 136.5 cm
Inscriptions: b.l. in embroidery floss, "Tuu'luq" (in syllabics)
Collection Edward and Naomi Bassuk, New York
(see text pp. 30, 36)

17
Ulu Women 1976
Felt, embroidery floss, and thread on duffle
146.0 x 146.0 cm
Government of Manitoba Art Collection, Winnipeg (037006)
(see text pp. 30, 32)

EXHIBITION
Tuu'luq/Anguhadluq, 1976 (no. 47 in catalogue, repr., n. p.)

PUBLICATIONS
Baker, 1980 (repr. p. 29)

18
Together in Spring 1977
Felt, embroidery floss, and thread on stroud
137.5 x 144.0 cm
Inscriptions: b.c. in embroidery floss, "Tuu'luq Marion" (in syllabics)
Collection Orville P. Speirs and Theresa Hass-Speirs, Winnipeg
(see text p. 34)

Exhibition
Marion Tuu'luq, 1980 (no. 28 in booklet, as *#1567*)

19
Laughing at Men with Big Noses 1978
Felt, embroidery floss, and thread on duffle
95.0 x 68.0 cm
Inscriptions: b.c. in embroidery floss, "Tuu'luq" (in syllabics)
Collection Allan and Faigie Waisman, Vancouver
(see text p. 32)

Exhibition
Marion Tuu'luq, 1980 (no. 21 in booklet, as *#3501*, col. repr., n. p.)

20
People, Shamans, and Spirits c. 1978
Felt, embroidery floss, and thread on duffle
158.0 x 152.0 cm
National Gallery of Canada, Ottawa. Gift of the Department of Indian Affairs and Northern Development, 1989 (36652)
(see text pp. 13, 39)

Exhibitions
In the Shadow of the Sun, 1988–90 (no. 273 in catalogue, as *Menschen, Schamanen und Geister* [People, Shamans, and Spirits], col. repr. p. 612)
Qamanittuaq: The Art of Baker Lake, 1991
Head and Face, 1996

21
Journey 1978
Felt, embroidery floss, and thread on stroud
142.0 x 112.0 cm
Inscriptions: b.c. in embroidery floss, "Marion Tuu'luq" (in syllabics)
Collection Dr. Arnold Richards and Dr. Arlene Kramer Richards, New York
(see text p. 39)

Exhibition
Marion Tuu'luq, 1980 (no. 7 in booklet as *#3631*, col. repr., n. p.)

22
Goose Hunting in Spring 1978
Felt, embroidery floss, and thread on stroud
140.0 x 150.0 cm
Inscriptions: b.c. in embroidery floss, "Tuu'luq" (in syllabics)
Private collection
(see text p. 30)

Exhibition
Marion Tuu'luq, 1980 (no. 2 in booklet, as *#2794*, col. repr., n. p.)

23
Imagining Trees 1978
Felt, embroidery floss, and thread on stroud
143.0 x 116.5 cm
Inscriptions: b.c. in embroidery floss, "Tuu'luq" (in syllabics)
Collection Earl and Laya Braemer, Winnipeg
(see text pp. 28, 36, 37)

Exhibition
Marion Tuu'luq, 1980 (no. 8 in booklet, as *#3401*, col. repr. on cover)

24
The Life of a Man c. 1978–79
Felt, embroidery floss, and thread on stroud
69.6 x 69.6 cm
Inscriptions: b.l. in embroidery floss, "Tuu'luq" (in syllabics)
Collection John and Joyce Price, Mercer Island, Washington
(see text p. 33)

25
Faces (from the story of Kiviuq and Iqupjuk) 1979
Felt, embroidery floss, and thread on stroud
80.5 x 74.5 cm
Inscriptions: b.c. in embroidery floss, "Tuu'luq" (in syllabics)
Art Gallery of Ontario, Toronto. Purchased with the assistance of the Joan Chalmers Inuit Art Purchase Fund, 1998 (98/180, formerly *Faces*)
(see text p. 38)

Exhibition
Northern Lights, 1993–94 (no. 33 in catalogue, as *Untitled*)

Publications
Driscoll, 1994 (col. repr. p. 10, as fig.12, *Untitled*)

26
Untitled 1979
Felt, embroidery floss, and thread on stroud
86.7 x 50.3 cm
Collection Carol Thrun and Glenn Littenberg, La Canada, California
(see text p. 30)

Exhibition
Marion Tuu'luq, 1980 (no. 16 in booklet, as *#6621*, col. repr., n. p.)

27
Bountiful Thoughts c. 1978–79
Felt, embroidery floss, and thread on stroud
70.0 x 76.3 cm
Inscriptions: b.c. in embroidery floss, “Tuu’luq” (in syllabics)
University of Alberta Art and Artifact Collection, Museums and Collections Services, Clifford E. Lee Collection of Inuit Wall Hangings, Edmonton (983.44.2, formerly *Untitled*)
(see text pp. 31, 32, 39)

EXHIBITIONS
Universiade ’83, 1983
Clifford E. Lee Collection, 1984
Marion Tuu’luq, 1990

28
Dismembered/Remembered
c. 1979–80
Felt, embroidery floss, and thread on stroud
69.9 x 75.7 cm
Inscriptions: b.r. in embroidery floss, “Tuu’luq” (in syllabics)
University of Alberta Art and Artifact Collection, Museums and Collections Services, Clifford E. Lee Collection of Inuit Wall Hangings, Edmonton (983.44.4, formerly *Untitled*)
(see text p. 33)

EXHIBITIONS
Universiade ’83, 1983
Marion Tuu’luq, 1990
Clifford E. Lee Collection, 1984
Worlds of the Inuit, 1999
Arctic Survival, 2001–02

29
Tele-Vision Spirits c. 1980
Felt, embroidery floss, on stroud
63.0 x 74.5 cm
Inscriptions: b.l. in embroidery floss, “Tuu’luq” (in syllabics)
Macdonald Stewart Art Centre Collection, Guelph. Purchased with funds raised by the Art Centre Volunteers, 1988 (MS1988.015, formerly *Untitled*)
(see text p. 41)

EXHIBITIONS
Spirit Imagery, 1997
Elagiiqniq: Inuit Art, 1995

30
Composition (large bird and figures) c. 1981
Felt, embroidery floss, and thread on stroud
71.5 x 75.0 cmz
Inscriptions: b.l. in embroidery floss, “Tuu’luq” (in syllabics)
Macdonald Stewart Art Centre Collection, Guelph. Purchased with funds raised by the Art Centre Volunteers, 1989 (MS1989.015, formerly *Untitled*)
(see text pp. 31, 32)

EXHIBITIONS
Spirit Imagery, 1997
Elagiiqniq: Inuit Art, 1995

31
Untitled c. 1983
Felt, embroidery floss, and thread on duffle
93.0 x 98.0 cm
Inscriptions: b.l. in embroidery floss, “Tuu’luq” (in syllabics)
Private collection
(see text p. 40)

32
Avaalaaqiaq (willows) 1985
Felt, embroidery floss and thread on stroud
70.7 x 74.2 cm
Inscriptions: b.l. in embroidery floss, “Tuu’luq” (in syllabics)
Canadian Museum of Civilization, Gatineau, Quebec (IV-C-5183)
(see text p. 37)

EXHIBITIONS
Inuit Art, 1992–93

PUBLICATIONS
Gautsche, 1993 (repr. p. 28)
Hessel, 1998, p. 174 (col. repr. p. 174, as pl. 140, *Untitled [Foliage]*)

33
One Man’s Dream 1988
Felt, embroidery floss, and thread on stroud
152.5 x 240.1 cm
Inscriptions: b.c. in embroidery floss, “Tuu’luq” (in syllabics); c.l. within image in embroidery floss, “taapsuma sinnaktuumania” (“one man’s dream”, in syllabics)
The Winnipeg Art Gallery, on loan from Marie Bouchard and James McLeod (WAG 20.96)
(see text pp. 13, 37)

EXHIBITIONS
Northern Lights, 1993–94 (no. 31 in catalogue, col. repr. p. 20)
Immaginario Inuit, 1995 (no. 138 in catalogue, col. repr. p. 232)
Winter Display, 1997–98

PUBLICATIONS
Driscoll, 1994 (col. repr. p. 13, as fig. 16)
Dickie, 1994 (col. repr. p. 30)

34
Tuu'luq and Her Family 1988
Felt, embroidery floss, and thread on stroud
150.0 x 206.0 cm
Inscriptions: b.l. within image, in embroidery floss, "Tuu'luq Marion" (in syllabics)
The Winnipeg Art Gallery, on loan from Marie Bouchard and James McLeod (WAG 28.96)
(see text pp. 21, 101)

Exhibition
The Family in Inuit Art, 1989 (no number in catalogue, col. repr. p. 27)

35
Untitled 1989
Felt and embroidery floss on stroud
137.0 x 110.0 cm
Inscriptions: b.c. in embroidery floss, "Tuu'luq" (syllabics)
Collection Robert and Irene Bilan, Winnipeg
(see text p. 21)

Exhibition
Northern Lights 1993–94 (no. 32, as *People of the Drum*)

36
The Prayer Meeting 1989
Felt, embroidery floss, and thread on stroud
143.0 x 120.0 cm
Inscriptions: b.l. in embroidery floss, "Tuu'luq Marion" (in syllabics)
The Winnipeg Art Gallery, on loan from Marie Bouchard and James Macleod (WAG 27.96)
(see text pp. 41, 101)

Exhibitions
Immaginario Inuit, 1995 (no. 147 in catalogue, col. repr. p. 240)
Colors from the Snow, 1996
R. C. A. Prairie Region, 1997–98 (listed in catalogue, no number, col. repr., n. p.).

Publication
Muehlen, 1992 (col. repr. p. 35)

37
Rites of Spring 1989
Felt, embroidery floss, and thread on stroud
145.0 x 152.0 cm
Inscriptions: b.l. in embroidery floss, "Tuu'luq" (in syllabics)
Private collection
(see text pp. 30, 101)

Exhibition
A Stitch in Time, 1997

Publication
Hancock, 1991 (repr. p. 38)

AFTERWORD

Phoebe Anne Kudja'aq wearing Tuu'luq's Expo '86 amauti and qarliik.
Photo: Marie Bouchard

MY NAME IS PHOEBE ANNE KUDJA'AQ and I am Marion Tuu'luq's granddaughter. On behalf of Tuu'luq's family, I would like to say a big thank you to everyone for making Tuu'luq feel so special with the exhibition of her wall hangings at the National Gallery in 2002. As I write this, my granny is about to celebrate her ninety-first birthday. I think the exhibition is giving her a reason to live.

Our friend Marie Bouchard, who used to live in Baker Lake, came back several times to discuss the exhibition with Tuu'luq and our family. She brought photos of my granny's wall hangings that she had found in museums, galleries, and private collections. There were over one hundred. Tuu'luq cried tears of happiness when she saw the pictures of her hangings and the people who had them — from all over Canada and the United States. Tuu'luq explained that she can't make pieces like that anymore. It was obvious to me how much she had enjoyed sewing these beautiful cloth pictures. She is very grateful to all those people she has never met who have her wall hangings.

I, too, have one of her hand-sewn items — an *amauti* (woman's parka) with *qarliik* (pants) made from brown and white artificial fur (known as "angel fur"). The amauti is made in the Baker-Lake style with insets of white fur sewn into the front and back of the garment and along the edge of the hood. Thin strips of dark fur are inset into this white fur to make a pleasing design. Red and white strips of bias tape decorate the shoulders and front of the amauti. In the olden days, these would have been made of different colours of fur. Around the bottom edge of the amauti is a fringe made of string. Fringes used to be made from caribou sinew. A woven belt with two big wooden disks covered in calico material wraps under the pouch of the amauti and ties in the front. This is so that a baby packed in the *amaut* (pouch) will not slip out. The pants are also decorated with a wide strip of white angel fur inset along the outer legs, with a thin orange strip of angel fur along the bottom. The pants come to just below the knee.

Tuu'luq wore this amauti to Expo '86 in Vancouver. Wherever she went, people admired her garment and wanted to have it. The same thing happened when my aunt Phillipa Iksiraq wore it to the Inuvik Arts Festival. But we haven't given it to anyone. We want to keep it in our family as a keepsake of Tuu'luq's beautiful sewing.

Tuu'luq was married twice, first to Ujarai, and then to the well-known artist Luke Anguhadluq. She had thirteen children with her first husband, only four of whom survive today — Barnabus Oosuaq, Thomas Iksiraq, Rosie Anguhadluq (my adoptive mother), and James Qingnaqtuq. Oosuaq and Iksiraq are well-known printmakers. With Anguhadluq, she had three children, but they all died. She and Anguhadluq adopted two children, Eva Nagyougalik and Tony Anguhadluq. Eva and her husband Paul look after my granny. Tuu'luq has twenty-six grandchildren, twenty-two great-grandchildren, and one great-great-grandchild.

I remember going to see my granny a lot when she was still sewing. She really wouldn't let anybody watch. She sewed in her room, where it was quiet and away from the children. Seated on her bed, she would spread out her material and start cutting and sewing the shapes onto the background. The embroidery took much longer and was best done in daylight. In the evenings, she liked to play cards and board games with her relatives and friends and to watch *Three's Company* on TV. At times she would go and visit her cousin Jessie Oonark. Oonark rarely left her house, because she was always busy sewing and drawing, so my granny would go there. They were good friends and liked to talk about the past and their lives today.

Even though I am quite busy with my two young children, I still visit my granny often. She can't walk anymore and is confined to her bed. She is very wise and is always happy to see my kids. I never knew that my granny had accomplished so much in her life. My youngest son is named Tuu'luq after her, so she will always be with us.

BAKER LAKE, FEBRUARY 2001

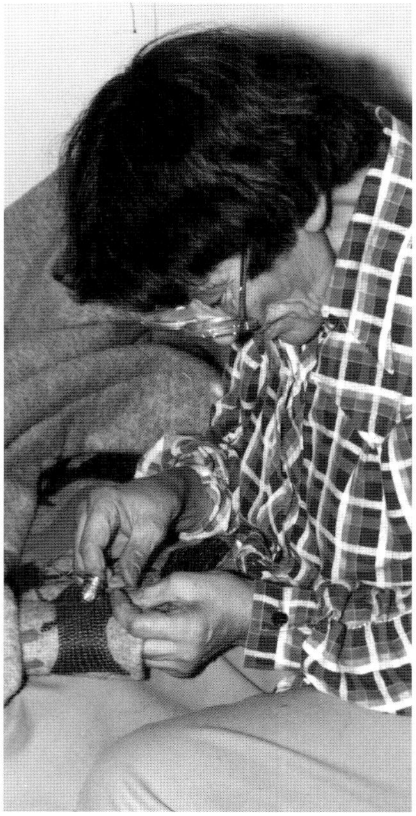

Tuu'luq at work in her room, 1985
Photo: NWT Archives, G-1990-007, Box 15

CHRONOLOGY

Tuu'luq with *Migration*, the work she created for Expo '86 in Vancouver.
Photo: NWT Archives, G-1990-007, Box 15

1910? Marion Tuu'luq is born at her family's camp at Innituuq, in the Utkuhiksalik area, near the coastal waters of Chantrey Inlet around 1910. (As Inuit did not record dates in this era, the exact year of birth is often unknown.) Within a year of her birth, her mother passes away, leaving her and two older brothers to be raised by their invalid father, grandparents, and other relatives. They remain in the area until Tuu'luq is about age seven. Although her exposure to coastal life is short, elements of the coastal Inuit's lifestyle and traditions inform her imagery in later years, particularly the importance of fish as a main source of food.

1920? When Tuu'luq is around ten, her father dies. She now lives with various families in the Back River/Garry Lake region to the northwest of Baker Lake. Her orphan status deprives her of a strong maternal figure on which to model herself. She learns where she can the women's skills essential for survival and teaches herself to cut and sew traditional clothing items.

1928? Late in her teens, Tuu'luq moves to her cousin Ujarai's camp, to be his wife. He is from the Back River area. Together, they have thirteen children, possibly fourteen, she is no longer certain. Only four survive to adulthood.

1939 An Anglican Minister visits Inuit in the Back River region in April, and baptizes Tuu'luq in an iglu.

1946 A landing strip is built on the ice at Baker Lake in February and the first DC3 airplane lands. Radio communication equipment is also installed at this time. In June, a landing strip is built on the ground.

1954 Tuu'luq's husband Ujarai dies mysteriously while out hunting in March, killed, some people say, by dwarves. It is a time of widespread hunger in the Back River/Garry Lake area. Inuit are forced to eat their dogs and boil old caribou bones for sustenance. Tuu'luq and her four-year-old daughter are severely ill. A relative offers shelter at his camp for her and her children. They continue to shift from camp to camp, not wishing to be a burden on any one family.

1955	Tuu'luq joins the widower Luke Anguhadluq at his camp and becomes his wife. Anguhadluq is a well-respected hunter and responsible for the well-being of a large number of people in his camp. They have three children together, none of whom survive. Tuu'luq and Anguhadluq move frequently to various camp sites along the Back River in search of caribou and fish, which remain scarce throughout the latter half of the 1950s.
1956–57	The settlement of Baker Lake begins to take its present shape. Formerly a Hudson's Bay Company trading post and Anglican and Catholic mission site, it receives a federally-built nursing station in 1956. Pre-fabricated government-subsidized housing starts to be constructed in the mid-1950s. A school is built in 1957. A handicraft project for Inuit women and young girls is started in 1957 by Edith Dodds, wife of federal Northern Services Officer and area administrator S. Dodds.
1961	Anguhadluq moves Tuu'luq and their family to the settlement of Baker Lake around this time so that the children can receive medical care and attend school. At the settlement, they continue to live in tents and iglus, and make several forays out into the surrounding area to search for land foods. Tuu'luq sews some traditional caribou skin clothing for the RCMP.
1961–62	William Larmour, a development officer with the Industrial Division, Department of Northern Affairs and National Resources, Ottawa, winters in Baker Lake and establishes the Kamanijjuak Craft Centre (also known as the Baker Lake Eskimo Craft Centre).
1963–65	In the spring of 1963, Gabriel (Gabe) Gély, a French artist then living in the Arctic, is hired as an arts and crafts officer for Baker Lake. Gély encourages the production of work in all media. The first exhibition of sculpture from Baker Lake, *Eskimo Carvers of Keewatin N. W. T.*, is held at the Winnipeg International Airport in 1964, under the sponsorship of The Winnipeg Art Gallery.
1966–67	Tuu'luq learns to make modern and traditional-style clothing out of wool duffle at a sewing project operated in 1966 and 1967 by Elizabeth Whitton, the wife of the Anglican minister at Baker Lake. She teaches herself to do embroidery by looking at embroidered motifs on peoples' clothing. Tuu'luq and other women in the project experiment with making small cloth pictures out of leftover scraps of material. In the mid-1960s, she also produces drawings at the invitation of the craft officer, Boris Kotelewetz.

1967 A federally funded sewing factory opens at Baker Lake in late 1967. Workers use industrial sewing machines to produce parkas and other clothing items. The project closes down shortly afterwards, opening again in 1969 as the Duffle Garment Shop, operated by the Government of the Northwest Territories. It closes in November 1970.

Tuu'luq travels to Winnipeg for lung surgery.

Tuu'luq and Anguhadluq are assigned their own house in Baker Lake.

Tuu'luq is again taken ill and flown to Churchill, Manitoba, for medical care.

1969 Art advisors Jack Butler and Sheila Butler arrive in Baker Lake in July 1969. With the assistance of Elizabeth Whitton, the Butlers revive women's sewing and handicrafts. Tuu'luq is invited to make clothing items – duffle vests, mitts, socks with embroidered designs. She also experiments with beads and creating necklace collars from beads, using leftover materials from the sewing factory. Two of these appear in the current exhibition (both 1969, cats. 1 and 2).

1970 The collection of Baker Lake prints is launched in Edmonton, Alberta, in April. These editioned prints are offered for sale through southern distributors.

1971–72 Tuu'luq produces two *atigiit* (women's inner parkas) decorated with beadwork designs. Her sewn items are meticulously stitched and richly decorated. She is invited to make works on cloth for the newly established Miqsuvik Sewing Centre at Baker Lake.

Reverend Armand Tagoona establishes an Arctic Christian Fellowship at Baker Lake. Tuu'luq attends these services as well as those at the Anglican church.

With the assistance of a $50,000 loan from the federal Eskimo Loan Fund, the Sanavik Co-operative is established in Baker Lake to coordinate the art activities in the settlement.

Tuu'luq produces works on cloth in the form of long, thin, vertical bands with embroidered designs. By 1972, she has developed a unique colour palette of intense earth colours, close in value. The earliest work on cloth found for the current exhibition dates from this period.

CBC television begins broadcasting to Baker Lake.

1972–73 Tuu'luq starts to add bright colours to her palette with dramatic effect. Jack Butler and Sheila Butler leave Baker Lake in 1972. Both continue to serve as art advisors for an additional year, commuting from Winnipeg. Jack Butler then continues on his own until 1976. Harold Etegoyuk remains as the manager of the Miqsuvik Sewing Centre.

For the next year, Tuu'luq experiments with embroidery and the linear aspects of sewing, paying particular attention to the positive and negative interplay of space on the picture surface.

1973–74 An exhibition of works on cloth by the women of Baker Lake takes place at the local Adult Education Centre in late autumn or early winter 1973. It is publicized in an article in the *Keewatin Echo* (January 1974).

Lake Trout (1973, cat. 5), one other untitled appliquéd-and-embroidered work on cloth, and an *atigi* by Tuu'luq are selected for the *Crafts from Arctic Canada* exhibition. Two prints of Tuu'luq's drawings also make their debut in the fourth edition of the annual Baker Lake Print Collection. Tuu'luq's drawings are included in an additional 12 editions between 1974 and 1990.

1976 This is a productive and busy year for Tuu'luq. She is featured in a two-person exhibition with her husband, *Tuu'luq/Anguahdluq*, organized by The Winnipeg Art Gallery. Others of her works appear simultaneously in a commercial exhibition titled *Anguhadluq/Tuu'luq: Husband and Wife of Baker Lake* at The Upstairs Gallery in Winnipeg. Tuu'luq attends the opening ceremonies for both. Public Works Canada commissions her to create a work on cloth for the Post Office in Penetanguishene, Ontario.

Jack Butler withdraws as art advisor to the artists of Baker Lake. The Miqsuvik Sewing Centre is now supervised by David Sutherland, Regional Arts and Crafts Officer for the Department of Economic Development, Government of the Northwest Territories. Tuu'luq now interacts primarily with the local manager of the centre, Harold Etegoyuk.

1977 Fire destroys the Sanavik Cooperative building and all its contents.

Tuu'luq's prints appear in several group exhibitions of Inuit art between 1977 and 1980.

1978 She is elected a member of the Royal Canadian Academy of Arts in November.

1979 *Keewatin Wallhangings* (1979–81), a touring exhibition organized by Canadian Arctic Producers, a southern marketing agency for Inuit art, includes one of her works on cloth.

1980 Tuu'luq's works on cloth are featured in a public group exhibition and three commercial gallery exhibitions in 1980. Her beaded *atigi* from 1971 is displayed in The Winnipeg Art Gallery's exhibition *The Inuit Amautik: I Like My Hood To Be Full.* Other works appear at the Theo Waddington Gallery in New York, the Inuit Gallery of Vancouver, and in a solo exhibition of her works on cloth at The Upstairs Gallery, Winnipeg.

For the next three years, prints of Tuu'luq's drawings are included in several national group exhibitions.

1982 In February Tuu'luq's husband, Luke Anguhadluq, dies.

1983–85 *Grasp Tight the Old Ways: Selections from the Klamer Family Collection of Inuit Art*, organized by the Art Gallery of Ontario, and presented in Toronto and touring from May 1983 to April 1985, features *Sun Woman* (1975, cat. 12).

The market for Baker-Lake works on cloth is weak. The Miqsuvik Sewing Centre accumulates a large deficit and backlog of unsold inventory.

Tuu'luq's drawings continue to be presented in national public exhibitions and also at commercial galleries over the next five years.

1986 Tuu'luq creates a work on cloth, *Migration* (see p. 96), for the Inuit pavilion at Expo '86, in Vancouver and attends the event. *Migration* is now in the collection of the Government of Nunavut.

1987 The Government of the Northwest Territories closes the Miqsuvik Sewing Centre in February and disposes of its assets, leaving the fabric artists of Baker Lake without a means to obtain material or sell their work.

Marie Bouchard, a resident of Baker Lake, establishes an arts-and-crafts shop and works as an independent art advisor to the Baker Lake artists, with a particular focus on reviving the making of works on cloth.

1988 The work on cloth *Untitled* (1976, cat. 15), now in the collection of the National Gallery of Canada, is included in the major touring international exhibition *In the Shadow of the Sun: Contemporary Indian and Inuit Art in Canada*, organized by the Canadian Museum of Civilization in Gatineau, Quebec.

1989 *Tuu'luq and Her Family* (1988, cat. 34) is included in the public exhibition *The Family in Inuit Art* at the McMullen Gallery, Edmonton.

Tuu'luq develops an increasingly troublesome skin allergy to wool, effectively ending her ability to work on cloth by the end of 1989. The last work she produces is *The Prayer Meeting* (1989, cat. 36).

1990 Tuu'luq receives an honorary Doctor of Laws Degree from the University of Alberta in June.

In October, Tuu'luq suffers a stroke with resulting weakness in her right hand and arm. She is no longer able to sew and draws with difficulty.

The Innuit Gallery of Eskimo Art, Toronto, mounts a Baker Lake wall-hanging show in November 1990. *Rites of Spring* (1989, cat. 37) is featured.

UNICEF selects Tuu'luq's work on cloth *Harmony between Man and Animals* (location unknown) as an illustration for its 1990 *North American Heritage* greeting-card series.

Tuu'luq with *Trumpeter Swans* at the 1973 exhibition *Baker Lake Wall Hangings and Vests*.

Photo: Stanley Zazelenchuk

1991–2002 Tuu'luq's works on cloth continue to be purchased for public and private collections of Inuit art, and presented in such national and international exhibitions as *Women of the North*, Vancouver, 1992; *Northern Lights,* Baltimore, 1993–94; *Immaginario Inuit,* Verona, Italy, 1995; *Colors from the Snow*, Oregon, 1996; *A Stitch in Time*, Toronto, 1997; *Spirit Imagery*, Waterloo, 1997; the *R. C. A. Prairie Region Exhibition*, Winnipeg, 1997, and Regina, 1998; *Worlds of the Inuit,* Edmonton, 1999; *Keewatin 2000*, Vancouver, 2000; and *Arctic Survival*, Edmonton, 2002.

Marie Bouchard leaves Baker Lake in June 1997.

Tuu'luq continues to live with her daughter and son-in-law Eva and Paul Nagyougalik at their home in Baker Lake, surrounded by family and friends.

2002–04 Marion Tuu'luq dies, at home in Baker Lake, on 22 September 2002.

The solo exhibition *Marion Tuu'luq* is held at the National Gallery of Canada from 11 October 2002 to 12 January 2003, featuring 37 works on cloth, accompanied by a fully illustrated colour catalogue in English and French editions. The exhibition tours until 2004.

EXHIBITIONS AND PUBLIC COLLECTIONS

This list includes selected solo, duo, and group exhibitions of Marion Tuu'luq's works on cloth. It does not cover the 13 Baker Lake print collections published between between 1974 and 1990 which included graphic work by Tuu'luq. Nor does it cover other exhibitions of her prints and drawings.

Solo and Duo Exhibitions

2002–04 *Marion Tuu'luq* (catalogue), National Gallery of Canada, Ottawa, 11 October 2002 — 12 January 2003. Tour: The Winnipeg Art Gallery, 21 August — 12 October 2003 / Art Gallery of Ontario, Toronto, 1 November 2003 — 11 January 2004 / Macdonald Stewart Art Centre, Guelph, 20 May — 29 July 2004.

1990 *Marion Tuu'luq and Baker Lake Wall Hangings*, Northern Alberta Jubilee Auditorium, University of Alberta, Edmonton, 25 May - 13 June 1990.

1980 *Marion Tuu'luq: Wallhangings* (booklet), The Upstairs Gallery, Winnipeg, 26 January — 9 February 1980.

Lukta, Cape Dorset Sculpture / Tuu'luq, Baker Lake Wallhangings, Drawings, Inuit Gallery of Vancouver, opened 8 December 1980.

1976 *Tuu'luq/Anguhadluq: An Exhibition of Works by Marion Tuu'luq and Luke Anguhadluq of Baker Lake* (catalogue), The Winnipeg Art Gallery, 10 September — 7 November 1976.

Anguhadluq/Tuu'luq: Husband and Wife of Baker Lake, The Upstairs Gallery, Winnipeg, 17–27 October 1976.

Selected Group Exhibitions

2001–02	*Arctic Survival*, University of Alberta Hospital, McMullen Gallery, Edmonton, 30 November 2001 - 30 January 2002.
2000	*Keewatin 2000* (catalogue), Spirit Wrestler Gallery, Vancouver, 29 April — 19 May 2000.
1999	*Worlds of the Inuit*, Provincial Museum of Alberta, Edmonton, 8 May — 6 September 1999.
1998–99	Permanent collection installation, National Gallery of Canada, Ottawa, 30 October 1998 — 21 March 1999.
1997–98	*The Royal Canadian Academy of Arts: Prairie Region Exhibition* (catalogue), organized by the R.C.A., [Winnipeg]. Tour: The Winnipeg Art Gallery, 30 May — 28 September 1997 / MacKenzie Art Gallery, Regina, 19 June — 16 August 1998.
	Winter Display, The Winnipeg Art Gallery, 16 December 1997 - 28 April 1998.
1997	*Spirit Imagery: Inuit Art from the Macdonald Stewart Art Centre Collection*, University of Waterloo Art Gallery, 16 January - 7 March 1997.
	A Stitch in Time: The History and Aesthetics of Baker Lake Wall Hangings, Textile Museum of Canada, Toronto, 3 May — 2 November 1997.
1996	*Head and Face: Selected Views in Inuit Sculpture*, National Gallery of Canada, Ottawa, 19 April — 3 November 1996 (works on cloth shown in conjunction with the exhibition).
	Colors from the Snow, Jensen Arctic Museum, Western Oregon University, Monmouth, Oregon, 14 June — 2 August 1996.
1995	*Immaginario Inuit: Arte e Cultura degli Esquimesi Canadesi* (catalogue), Gallerie d'Arte Moderna e Contemporanea di Palazzo Forti, Verona, Italy, organized by the Palazzo Forti, in collaboration with Arctic Cooperatives, Winnipeg, Giocoloco Communications, Toronto, and The Winnipeg Art Gallery, 19 March — 9 July 1995.
	Elagiiqniq: Inuit Art from the Collection, MacDonald Stewart Art Centre, Guelph, 28 April — 11 June 1995.
1994	*A University Collects: Recent Acquisitions*, Ring House Gallery, University of Alberta, Edmonton, 17 February — 11 March 1994.
	Between Worlds, Richmond Art Gallery, British Columbia, 7 July — 8 August 1994.
1993–94	*Northern Lights: Inuit Textile Art from the Canadian Arctic* (catalogue), Baltimore Museum of Art, 17 November 1993 — 30 January 1994. Tour: Macdonald Stewart Art Centre, Guelph, 11 June — 18 July 1994 / The Winnipeg Art Gallery, 17 August — 9 October 1994.

1992–93 *Inuit Art: Tradition and Regeneration*, Canadian Museum of Civilization, Gatineau, Quebec, 17 December 1992 — 2 May 1993.

1992 *Women of the North: An Exhibition of Art by Inuit Women of the Canadian Arctic* (catalogue), Marion Scott Gallery, Vancouver, 6 June — 11 July 1992.

1991 *Qamanittuaq: The Art of Baker Lake*, National Gallery of Canada, Ottawa, 3 June — 10 November 1991.

Sananguaq: The Swinton Collection of Inuit Art, Art Gallery of Ontario, Toronto, 27 March — 26 May 1991.

1990 *Baker Lake Wallhangings*, The Innuit Gallery of Eskimo Art, Toronto, 24 November — December 1990.

1989 *The Family in Inuit Art: An Exhibition of Inuit Carvings, Prints, and Wallhangings in Celebration of the Tenth Anniversary of the Inuit Art Enthusiasts* (catalogue), University of Alberta Hospital, McMullen Gallery, Edmonton, June — August 1989.

1988–90 *In the Shadow of the Sun: Contemporary Indian and Inuit Art in Canada / Im Schatten der Sonne: Zeitgenössische Kunst der Indianer und Eskimos in Kanada* (catalogue, published by CMC in 1988, in German), organized by the Canadian Museum of Civilization, Gatineau, Quebec, in conjunction with the University of Würzburg, West Germany. Tour: Museum für Kunst und Kulturgeschichte, and Museum am Ostwall, Dortmund, West Germany, 9 December 1988 — 28 February 1989 / Canadian Museum of Civilization, Gatineau, Quebec, 26 June — 31 December 1989 / Art Gallery of Nova Scotia, Halifax, 20 April — 24 June 1990.

1988 *Celebration of the Human Spirit*, organized from the University of Alberta Art and Artifact Collection for the festival "The Works: A Visual Art Celebration", Third Floor Galleries, Manulife Place, Edmonton, 30 June — 10 July 1988.

1987 *Winnipeg Collects: Inuit Art from Private Collections* (catalogue), The Winnipeg Art Gallery, 1 March — 26 July 1987.

1986 Expo '86, exhibition at the Inuit pavilion, Vancouver, 2 May - 13 October 1986.

1985 *Inuit Art in Edmonton Collections*, Edmonton Art Gallery, 3 January — 4 March 1985.

1984 The Clifford E. Lee Collection of Inuit Wall Hangings, organized by the Ring House Gallery, University of Alberta, Edmonton. Tour: Morris and Helen Belkin Art Gallery [formerly Fine Arts Gallery], University of British Columbia, Vancouver, 18 September - 13 October 1984.

1983–85 *Grasp Tight the Old Ways: Selections from the Klamer Family Collection of Inuit Art* (catalogue), Art Gallery of Ontario, Toronto, 27 May - 31 July 1983. Tour: The Winnipeg Art Gallery, 10 November 1983 - 2 January 1984 / Field Museum of Natural History, Chicago, 27 February - 27 May 1984 / Glenbow Museum, Calgary, 20 June - 15 August 1984 / Art Gallery of Greater Victoria, Victoria, 13 September - 21 October 1984 / McCord Museum, Montreal, 15 November 1984 — 13 January 1985 / Confederation Centre Art Gallery and Museum, Charlottetown, 21 February — 7 April 1985.

1983 *Universiade '83*, Edmonton Convention Centre, 28 June — 12 July 1983.

1980 *Wall Hangings by Various Artists*, selection of works on cloth for sale, Theo Waddington Galleries, New York, 7 June — 10 July 1980.

The Inuit Amautik: I Like My Hood To Be Full (catalogue), The Winnipeg Art Gallery, 9 August — 26 October 1980.

1979–80 *Keewatin Wallhangings 1979 –1981*, Canadian Arctic Producers, Ottawa. Tour: McMichael Canadian Art Collection, Kleinburg, 23 June - 16 September 1979; Mount Saint Vincent University Art Gallery, Halifax, 21 September — 4 October 1979; Place Bonaventure, Montreal, 1980.

1977 An exhibition of wall hangings at Kamanituak Public School, Baker Lake, Nunavut, May 1977.

1976 Olympic Games, Government of the Northwest Territories display, Montreal, July-August 1976.

1974 *Crafts from Arctic Canada* (catalogue), organized by the Canadian Eskimo Arts Council, Ottawa. Tour: Observation Gallery, Toronto-Dominion Centre, Toronto, 18 June — 15 August 1974 / National Museum of Man, Ottawa, 3 October — 1 December 1974.

1973 *Baker Lake Wallhangings and Vests*, Adult Education Centre, Baker Lake, Nunavut, winter 1973.

Public Collections

Art Gallery of Ontario, Toronto

Bank of Montreal, Toronto

Canada Post Penetanguishene, Ontario

Canadian Arctic Producers Ltd., Winnipeg

Canada Council Art Bank, Ottawa

Canadian Museum of Civilization, Gatineau, Quebec

Glenbow Museum, Calgary

Government of Manitoba, Winnipeg

Government of Nunavut, Iqaluit

Legislative Assembly of the Northwest Territories, Yellowknife

Macdonald Stewart Art Centre, Guelph

National Gallery of Canada, Ottawa

Prince of Wales Northern Heritage Centre, Yellowknife

The Winnipeg Art Gallery, Winnipeg

University of Alberta, Art and Artifact Collection, Edmonton

SELECTED BIBLIOGRAPHY

Baker, Marilyn. "The Tapestries of Marion Tuu'luq." *Branching Out*, 7:2 (1980), pp. 29–32.

_____. "Tapestries Reveal Human Will." *Winnipeg Free Press*, 31 January 1980.

Bhabha, Homi K. *The Location of Culture*. London / New York: Routledge, 1994.

Blodgett, Jean. *Tuu'luq/Anguhadluq: An Exhibition of Works by Marion Tuu'luq and Luke Anguhadluq of Baker Lake*. Winnipeg: The Winnipeg Art Gallery, 1976 (exhibition catalogue).

_____. *The Coming and Going of the Shaman: Eskimo Shamanism and Art*. Winnipeg: The Winnipeg Art Gallery, 1978 (exhibition catalogue).

_____. *Kenojuak*. Toronto: Firefly Books, 1985.

_____, and Marie Bouchard. *Jessie Oonark: A Retrospective*. Winnipeg: The Winnipeg Art Gallery, 1986 (exhibition catalogue).

Botkin, Daniel, and Edward A. Keller. *Environmental Science: Earth as a Living Planet*. New York / Chichester / Brisbane / Toronto / Singapore: John Wiley and Sons, 1994.

Bouchard, Marie. "The Baker Lake Story: Preserving the Inuit Way." *Piecework*, 3:2 (March/April 1995), pp. 79–81.

_____. "Marion Tuu'luq." In *North American Women Artists of the Twentieth Century: A Biographical Dictionary*, edited by Jules Heller and Nancy G. Heller, p. 549. New York / London: Garland Publishing, 1995.

_____. *An Inuit Perspective: Baker Lake Sculpture*. Baker Lake / Toronto: Itsarnittakarvik: Inuit Heritage Centre / Art Gallery of Ontario, 2000 (exhibition catalogue).

_____. *The Power of Thought: The Prints of Jessie Oonark*. Richmond, Virginia: University of Virginia, The Marsh Art Gallery, 2001 (exhibition catalogue).

Brydon, Diana. "The White Inuit Speaks: Contamination as Literary Strategy." In *Past the Last Post: Theorizing Post-Colonialism and Post-Modernism*, edited by Ian Adam and Helen Tiffin. Calgary: University of Calgary Press, 1990.

Butler, K. J. Unpublished transcript of interview with Jean Blodgett, 15 July 1976. On file at The Winnipeg Art Gallery.

_____. "My Visual Art Practice: Its Social Value." In *Fate Maps*, pp. 23–29. Peterborough: Art Gallery of Peterborough, 1999.

_____. Personal conversation with Marie Bouchard, Winnipeg, April 1999.

_____. "The 'Story Bones'." In *The Butler Collection: Early Baker Lake Drawings*, pp. 8–9. Toronto: Feheley Fine Arts, 1999.

Butler, Sheila. "Wall Hangings from Baker Lake." *The Beaver* (fall 1972), pp. 26–31.

_____. "Inuit Art: An Art of Acculturation." In *The First Passionate Collector: The Ian Lindsay Collection of Inuit Art*, by Darlene Wight, pp. 33–42. Winnipeg: The Winnipeg Art Gallery, 1991 (exhibition catalogue).

_____. "Baker Lake Revisited." *C Magazine*, no. 45 (spring 1995), pp. 22–33.

Canadian Inuit Art Information Centre, Tuu'luq biography file. Department of Indian Affairs and Northern Development, Gatineau, Quebec.

Cook, Cynthia. "Northern Lights: Inuit Textile Art from the Canadian Arctic – A Review Essay." *Inuit Art Quarterly*, 9:4 (winter 1994), pp. 44–49.

Crafts from Arctic Canada. [Ottawa]: Canadian Eskimo Arts Council, [1974] (exhibition catalogue).

Dickie, Bonnie. "Marie Bouchard and the Baker Lake Renaissance." *Up Here* (September / October 1994), pp. 28–32.

Dorais, Jacques-Louis. *Inuit Uqausiqatigiit: Inuit Languages and Dialects*. Iqaluit: Arctic College–Nunatta Campus, 1990.

Driscoll, Bernadette. *The Inuit Amautik: I Like My Hood To Be Full*. Winnipeg: The Winnipeg Art Gallery, 1980 (exhibition catalogue).

———. "A Woman's Vision, A Woman's Voice: Inuit Textile Art from Arctic Canada." *Inuit Art Quarterly*, 9:2 (summer 1994), pp. 4–13.

Eskimo Carvers of Keewatin, N. W. T. With essays by Ferdinand Eckhardt and William Larmour. Winnipeg: The Winnipeg Art Gallery, 1964 (exhibition catalogue).

Fernstrom, Katharine W., and Anita E. Jones. *Northern Lights: Inuit Textile Art from the Canadian Arctic*. Baltimore: The Baltimore Museum of Art, [1993] (exhibition catalogue).

Fleming, Marie. *Joyce Wieland*. Toronto: Art Gallery of Ontario / Key Porter Books, 1987 (exhibition catalogue).

Gautsche, Nancy. "Tradition and Regeneration," *Inuit Art Quarterly*, 8:2 (summer 1993), pp. 26–31.

Grande, John K. *Balance: Art and Nature*. Montreal / New York / London: Black Rose Books, 1994.

Hancock, Lyn. "The Artists of the NWT." *Above & Beyond* (winter 1991), pp. 37–38.

Hannan, Eleanor. "Marion Tuu'luq Wallhangings at Upstairs Gallery, January 26 – February 9." *Artmagazine* (May / June 1980), pp. 57–59.

Hessel, Ingo. *Inuit Art: An Introduction*. Vancouver / Toronto: Douglas and McIntyre, 1998.

"Honorary Degree for Friends' Nominee, Marion Tuu'luuq." *Friends of the University of Alberta Museums Newsletter* (spring 1990).

Ingram, Mathew. "From Igloo to Art Gallery." *Alberta Report* (June 1990), p. 49.

Inuit Broadcasting Corporation. Interview with Marion Tuu'luq and Ruth Qaullaryuk Nuilalik, November 1992, aired in Baker Lake.

"Inuit Artist Receives Doctorate." *Edmonton Journal*, 8 June 1990.

James, Geoffrey. "Northern Delights." *Time*, 103:26 (July 1974), p. 10.

Kreelak, Martin, and Olé Gjerstad. *Amarok's Song: The Journey to Nunavut* (film). National Film Board of Canada, 1991.

Lopez, Barry. *Arctic Dreams: Imagination and Desire in a Northern Landscape*. Toronto / New York / London / Sydney / Auckland: Bantam Books, 1987.

MacDonald, John. *The Arctic Sky: Inuit Astronomy, Star Lore, and Legend*. Toronto / Iqaluit: Royal Ontario Museum / Nunavut Research Institute, 1998.

MacKay, Gillian. "Eskimo Art: Elegance and Big Business." *The Whig Standard* (Kingston, Ontario), 6 August 1976.

Martin, Lee-Ann. "Negotiating Space for Aboriginal Art." In *On Aboriginal Representation in the Gallery*, edited by Lynda Jessup with Shannon Bagg. Mercury Series, Canadian Ethnology Service, Paper 135. Gatineau, Quebec: Canadian Museum of Civilization, 2002.

McMaster, Gerald. "Inter Alia: An Interview." *Harbour*, 3:1 (winter 1993–94), pp. 13–18.

———. "Our (Inter) Related History." In *On Aboriginal Representation in the Gallery*, edited by Lynda Jessup with Shannon Bagg. Mercury Series, Canadian Ethnology Service, Paper 135. Gatineau, Quebec: Canadian Museum of Civilization, 2002.

Michaels, Eric. *Bad Aboriginal Art: Tradition, Media, and Technological Horizons*, Theory Out of Bounds, vol. 3. Minneapolis: University of Minnesota Press, 1994.

Muehlen, Maria. "Baker Lake Wall-hangings: Starting from Scraps." *Inuit Art Quarterly*, 4:2 (spring 1989), pp. 6–11.

———. "Some Recent Work by Women of Baker Lake." *Inuit Art Quarterly*, 7:3 (summer / fall 1992), pp. 30–35.

Nemiroff, Diana, Robert Houle, and Charlotte Townsend-Gault. *Land Spirit Power: First Nations at the National Gallery of Canada*. Ottawa: National Gallery of Canada, 1992 (exhibition catalogue).

Newlands, Anne. *Canadian Art: From Its Beginnings to 2000*. Willowdale, Ontario / Buffalo, New York: Firefly, 2000.

Noah, William. "Starvation on the Land and My Experience in Baker Lake." In *Qamanittuaq – Where the River Widens: Drawings by Baker Lake Artists*, by Marion Jackson, Judith Nasby, and William Noah, pp.16–22. Guelph: Macdonald Stewart Art Centre, 1995.

Northward Journal 23: The Arctic Issue. Moonbeam (Manotick since 1996), Ontario: Penumbra Press, 1981, pp. 22–23.

Parker, Rozsika. *The Subversive Stitch: Embroidery and the Making of the Feminine*. New York: Routledge, 1989.

"People." *About Arts & Crafts* (winter 1978), p. 28.

Snyder, L. L. *Arctic Birds of Canada*. Toronto: University of Toronto Press, 1957.

Sutherland, David. Letter to Susan Mah, Canadian Arctic Producers, Ottawa, 3 December 1976. In author's file.

_____. Personal conversation with Marie Bouchard, 29 October 2000.

Teitelbaum, Matthew. "The Mourner's Cry: Some Thoughts about the Early Work of Betty Goodwin." In *The Art of Betty Goodwin*, edited by Jessica Bradley and Matthew Teitelbaum, pp. 7-35. Vancouver / Toronto: Art Gallery of Ontario / Douglas and McIntyre, 1998 (exhibition catalogue).

Tester, Frank James, and Peter Kulchyski. *Tammarnitt (Mistakes): Inuit Relocation in the Eastern Arctic 1939–63.* Vancouver: University of British Columbia Press, 1994.

Tuu'luq, Marion. "Stories by Marion Anguhadluq," illustrated by Germaine Arnaktuauyok. In *Northern People*, edited by David Webster, pp. 27-33. Yellowknife: Department of Information, Government of the Northwest Territories, 1975.

_____. "A Story of Starvation," translated by Susan Tagoona. *Inuit Today*, 6:9 (1977), pp. 26-31.

_____. "Marian Tulluq Angohalluq." In *Inuit Nunamiut: Inland Inuit*, edited by Mannik, Hattie, pp. 44-57. Baker Lake, Nunavut: Printed by Friesen, Canada. 1989.

Vastokas, Joan M. "Continuities in Eskimo Graphic Style." *Artscanada* (December 1971 / January 1972), pp. 69-83.

Wray, Gordon. "Members' Statement on Honorary Doctor of Laws for Marion Tuu'luuq." Hansard Official Report, Legislative Assembly of the Northwest Territories, 6th Session, 11th Assembly, Day 32 (5 April 1990), p. 729.

Zazelenchuk, Stanley. "Art Show." *Keewatin Echo*, no. 66 (January 1974), p. 2.

_____. Personal conversation with Marie Routledge, National Gallery of Canada, September 2001.